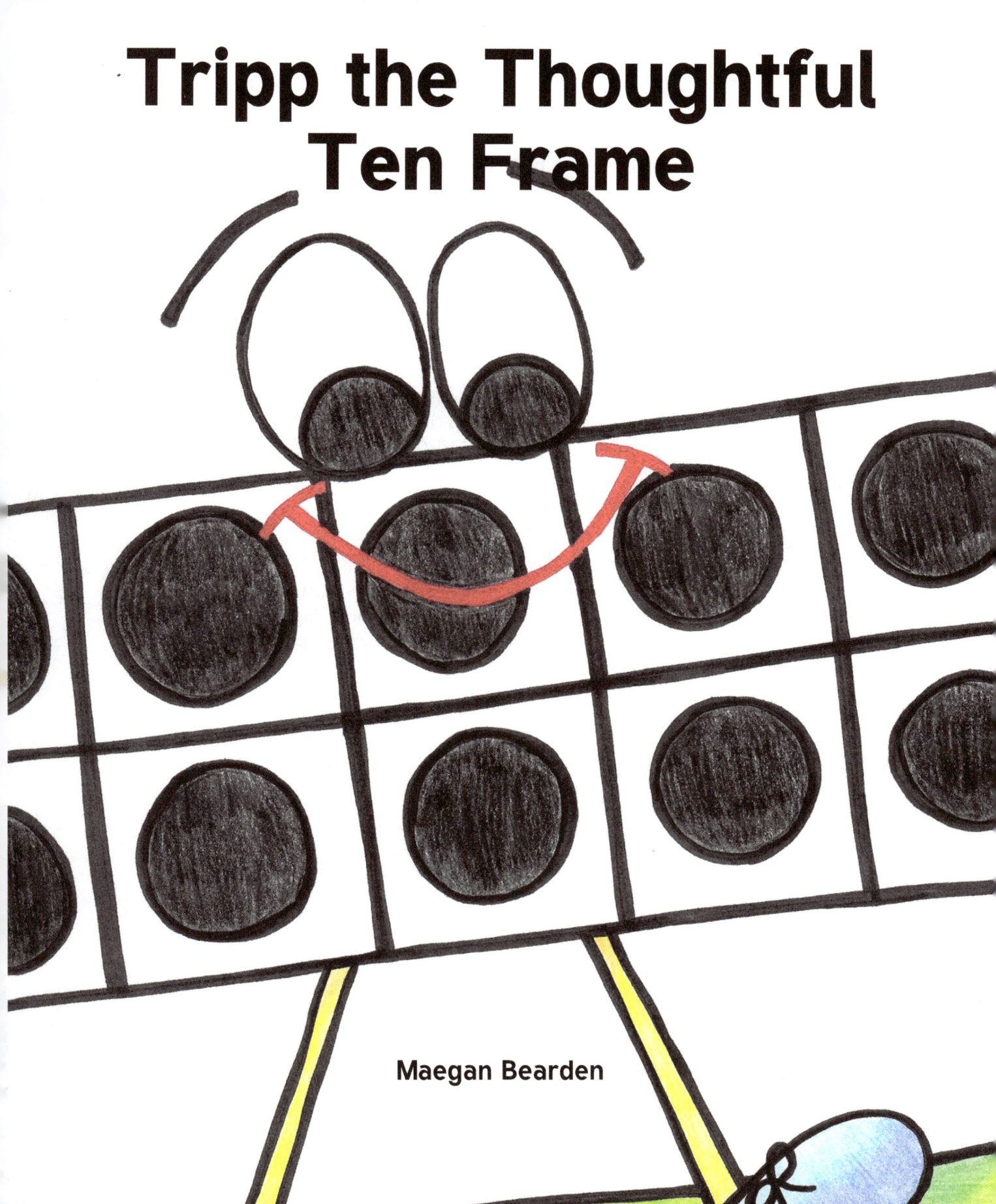

Tripp the Thoughtful
Ten Frame

Maegan Bearden

ISBN 979-8-89309-271-4 (Paperback)
ISBN 979-8-89309-273-8 (Hardcover)
ISBN 979-8-89309-272-1 (Digital)

Covenant Books
11661 Hwy 707
Murrells Inlet, SC 29576
www.covenantbooks.com

To my three little loves.

Tripp was a ten frame. But he wasn't an ordinary ten frame. He was a thoughtful ten frame with a special job. He worked every day keeping everyone's ten frames full at his station using his tank.

   He was on his way to work one morning and ran into a tiny ten frame. The tiny ten frame was sad. "Why are you sad?" asked Tripp.
   "I do not have many counters like my friends," said the tiny ten frame.
   "I'm sorry," said Tripp. "How many do you have?" asked Tripp.
   "Let's count them together. One, two, three, four, five, six, seven... seven counters in my ten frame," said the tiny ten frame.

"I have a full ten frame. Would you like a few of mine?" Tripp took three of his counters and gave them to his new friend.

"I only had seven counters. Now I have ten! Thank you!" screamed the tiny ten frame.

Tripp was excited for his new friend and continued on his way to work. Tripp opened up his station for a day of hard work and made sure his tank was ready to fill ten frames.

He looked down and remembered that he had given away three counters to the tiny ten frame. He wanted to be full to start the day, so he added three counters from the tank to fill his ten frame.

His first customer was Tucker. Tucker said, "I need my frame filled to ten, please. I am only at six counters."

"Of course," said Tripp.

"Let's fill you up with my tank! How many more will you need to be full? Let's count and see. One, two, three, four. You need 4 more." Tripp filled his frame up, and he was on his way.

Theo came walking down the street. "Tripp, I am only half full! My top row has all five counters, but my bottom row is completely empty. What should I do?" said Theo.

"I can help!" said Tripp. "You have five counters, so let's fill up your ten frame from my tank and you will be good to go. You need five more to be completely full," said Tripp.

The next customer's frame was almost empty. Tina only had two left. Tripp filled up the ten frame, and now she was full again.

Tripp was having a busy day, but was so thankful to be able to help others.

Tess was next to visit the station as she was almost empty at a number one.
"I am running on fumes and need some help with a fill-up!" said Tess.
"I've got it covered! Let's count together as we fill you up!"

"One, two, three, four, five, six, seven, eight, nine," said Tripp as he filled up her ten frame.

"Whew! We had to add nine this time. Thank you so much!" said Tess.

The last person to come by the station that day was Timmy. Timmy had four counters and was so happy to see Tripp was still at the station. "Hi, Tripp. Can you fill me up?" said Timmy.

"Of course, it looks like you need six more to be a full ten frame again," Tripp said.

"Thanks, Tripp. I feel so much better."
"Have a great night," said Tripp as Timmy left the station.

Tripp had completed a day's work and was ready to head home. Tripp the thoughtful ten frame was tired. On his walk home, he thought about all of his friends that he saw today and was able to help fill their ten frames. He thought how blessed he was to always feel full and what a joy it was to help his friends!

Printed in the USA
CPSIA information can be obtained
at www.ICGtesting.com
CBHW062341121024
15568CB00088B/97